Contents

T0351685

Written by
Diana Bentley
Sylvia Karavis
Illustrated by
Peter Richardson

Series editor **Dee Reid**

Heinemann
Part of Pearson

Characters

Agent
Em

Agent
Vee

Agent
Que

Agent
Zed

Twister

Tricky words

- suddenly
- crackled
- appeared
- destroy

- centre
- screamed
- reach
- vanished

Read these words to the student. Help them with these words when they appear in the text.

Introduction

The four agents were in their Base when suddenly all the alarms went off and an evil face appeared on their screen. It is Twister, the super-villain, who plans to smash cities to the ground with his tornado. He tells the agents that he will turn them to dust if they try to stop him. Vee has a plan to climb up inside Twister's tornado but will her plan work?

TWISTER

The agents were in the Base when suddenly the alarms went off.

Then the blank screen crackled into life and an evil face appeared.

"I am Twister.
I destroy everything in my path with my tornado.
I smash cities to the ground.
If you try to stop me I will turn you into dust."

Then the screen went blank.

"Can Twister really smash cities to the ground?" said Que.

"Yes, he can," said Vee. "He can destroy everything in his path. But we must try to stop him."
"How can we do that?" said Zed.

"Twister spins to make his tornado," said Vee. "We must hide in the old mine. Then when Twister is above us, we will climb up into the centre where he spins and stop him."

The agents hid in the mine.
They saw dust flying above them,
then everything went dark.

"The centre of the tornado is above us," said Vee. "We must attack now!"

The agents climbed up out of the mine into the centre of the tornado. They could see Twister turning the tornado above them.

Suddenly Que was sucked up into the tornado. "Que!" screamed Zed, but he could not reach him.

Twister looked down and saw
Zed reaching for Que.
"You cannot stop me," roared Twister.
"Get ready to be turned into dust!"

But just then Twister felt the tornado slow down.
He looked down.

The other agents had tied an old rope from the mine to Twister.
As he turned, the rope twisted and pulled him down into the mine.

"I will turn you into dust," said Twister again.
"I don't think so," said Vee. "You're the one
that is turning into dust!"
"I will be back!" screamed Twister as he
vanished into the mine.

"What about Que?" said Zed.
But as the tornado stopped twisting,
Que fell down and landed on Em.

"Good of you to drop in!" laughed Zed.
"Ha! Ha!" said Que.

"Twister is gone for now," said Vee. "But there are others who will try to destroy the world. We must be ready for them."

Quiz ////////////////////////

Text comprehension

Literal comprehension
p4 What was Twister's plan?
p6 What was Vee's plan?

Inferential comprehension
p10 How did Vee's plan nearly go wrong?
p14 How do you know Twister is still a risk to the world?
p15 How can you tell the agents like to joke?

Personal response
- Do you think the agents were brave?
- Do you think Twister will be back?

Word knowledge

p7 Find a compound word.
p10 Which verb has the author used instead of 'said'?
p15 Why is there an exclamation mark after Zed's words?

Spelling challenge

Read these words:

where   wish   eat

Now try to spell them!

Ha! Ha! Ha!

What is a tornado's favourite game?

Twister!

17

Find out about

- how tornadoes cause a lot of damage and sometimes pick up some surprising things.

Tricky words

- tornadoes
- spiral
- cause
- damage
- countries
- twisting
- raining
- thunderstorm

Read these words to the student. Help them with these words when they appear in the text

Introduction

Tornadoes are spirals of wind. They can move at speeds of over 120 miles an hour and they twist and turn as they move. Tornadoes cause a lot of damage. Sometimes small animals can get sucked up into a twisting tornado. When this happens it seems as if it is raining animals!

TORNADOES

Tornadoes are spirals of wind.
They can move at speeds of
over 120 miles an hour and they
twist and turn as they move.
Tornadoes cause a lot of damage.

Some countries have
very big tornadoes.

In big tornadoes
houses are blown down
and people are killed.

Tornadoes in the UK are very small
but there are lots of them!
There are about 33 small tornadoes in
the UK every year.
Even small tornadoes can cause a lot
of damage.

In 2005 there was a tornado in Birmingham. Lots of houses had their roofs blown off and their windows blown in.

Cars were over-turned.

No-one was killed but 19 people were hurt and 1000 trees were blown down.

Sometimes small animals can get sucked up
into a twisting tornado. The spiral of wind
holds the animals for a few minutes,
then it drops them back down to earth.
When this happens it seems as if it is raining animals

Raining frogs

In 1995 a family were driving along
a road in Scotland. It was raining
but then they saw that it was not
raindrops that were falling on the car.
Hundreds of tiny frogs were dropping
out of the sky!

At first no-one would believe them.
No-one thought frogs could
drop out of the sky.
Then they saw that there were
hundreds of tiny frogs on the road.
A small tornado had sucked up the
frogs from a lake and dropped them
on the car.

Raining fish

In 2000 there was a big thunderstorm
in Norfolk. After the thunderstorm,
people saw lots of dead fish
all over their gardens.

A tornado out at sea had
sucked up the fish.
When it twisted over the land, it
dropped the fish into the gardens.

Raining birds

In 2010 over a hundred dead birds dropped out of the sky into a garden in Somerset. A tornado had sucked up the birds into the clouds. The birds had died of the cold and then dropped into the garden.

When it pours with rain we say,
"It's raining cats and dogs!"
Perhaps we should say,
"It's raining fish and frogs!"

Quiz /////////////////////

Text comprehension

Literal comprehension
p19 How fast can a tornado move?
p22 Are there tornadoes in the UK?

Inferential comprehension
p21 How do tornadoes cause so much damage?
p23 Do you think the people in Birmingham in 2005 thought it was just a small tornado? Why not?
p27 Why do you think it was just the tiny frogs that were picked up by the tornado?

Personal response
• What do you think the family said when they saw frogs on their car?
• Some people try to get as close to a tornado as they can. Would you do that?

Word knowledge

p19 Find three words in the word 'tornadoes'.
p19 Find a word that means 'harm'.
p29 Find three verbs.

Spelling challenge

Read these words: **would   right   first**
Now try to spell them!

Ha! Ha! Ha!

What happens when it rains cats and dogs?
You have to be careful not to step in a poodle!